CHERRY WOOD IS HAPPY AGAIN!

JOYCE MARRIE, Ph.D.

Cherry Wood is Happy Again! © copyright 2020
Dr. Joyce Marrie
Published by, Chloe Arts and Publishing, LLC
Richfield MN. 55423

ISBN: 978-1-7358122-36

Copyright: Library of Congress: 1-10124057801

Illustrator: Ogbru Evidence

Printed in USA

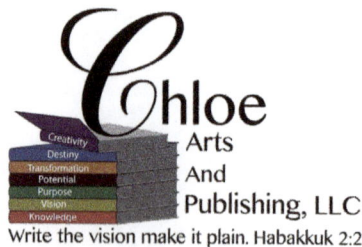

Chloe Arts And Publishing, LLC
Write the vision make it plain. Habakkuk 2:2

INTRODUCTION

Cherry Wood is Happy Again, is written by Dr. Joyce Marrie as part of a series of books which demonstrate a message of hope in times of despair.

Cherry Wood is Happy Again, a children's storybook, is taken from the experience of a young 6-year-old child, who was traumatized after seeing a media story on the George Floyd incident in Minneapolis. The story illustrates how a character (Cherry Wood the tree) copes with trauma after witnessing a brutal attack.

We know that George Floyd was treated horrifically and that fact has caused trauma to innumerable persons, including children, as they see the crime continuously replayed in the media.

This book can be used as a tool to reach children in a non-threatening way. Trauma is difficult for children to deal with, and this story gives them a way to relate to it, a way to experience a safe space and start healing.

The books *Cherry Wood Finds a Home* and *A Birthday Celebration for Cherry Wood* are tools to help deal with bullying, by demonstrating healthy friendships, and supporting healthy self-esteem in adverse situations.

The Cherry Wood series is a great tool for teachers, families, and therapists to reach troubled children. These stories also teach children to have empathy for others.

DEDICATION

This book was inspired by Justin P. Moore

One day Cherry Wood was on his way to visit his three tree friends. He was happy and looking forward to playing, singing, and dancing with his friends.

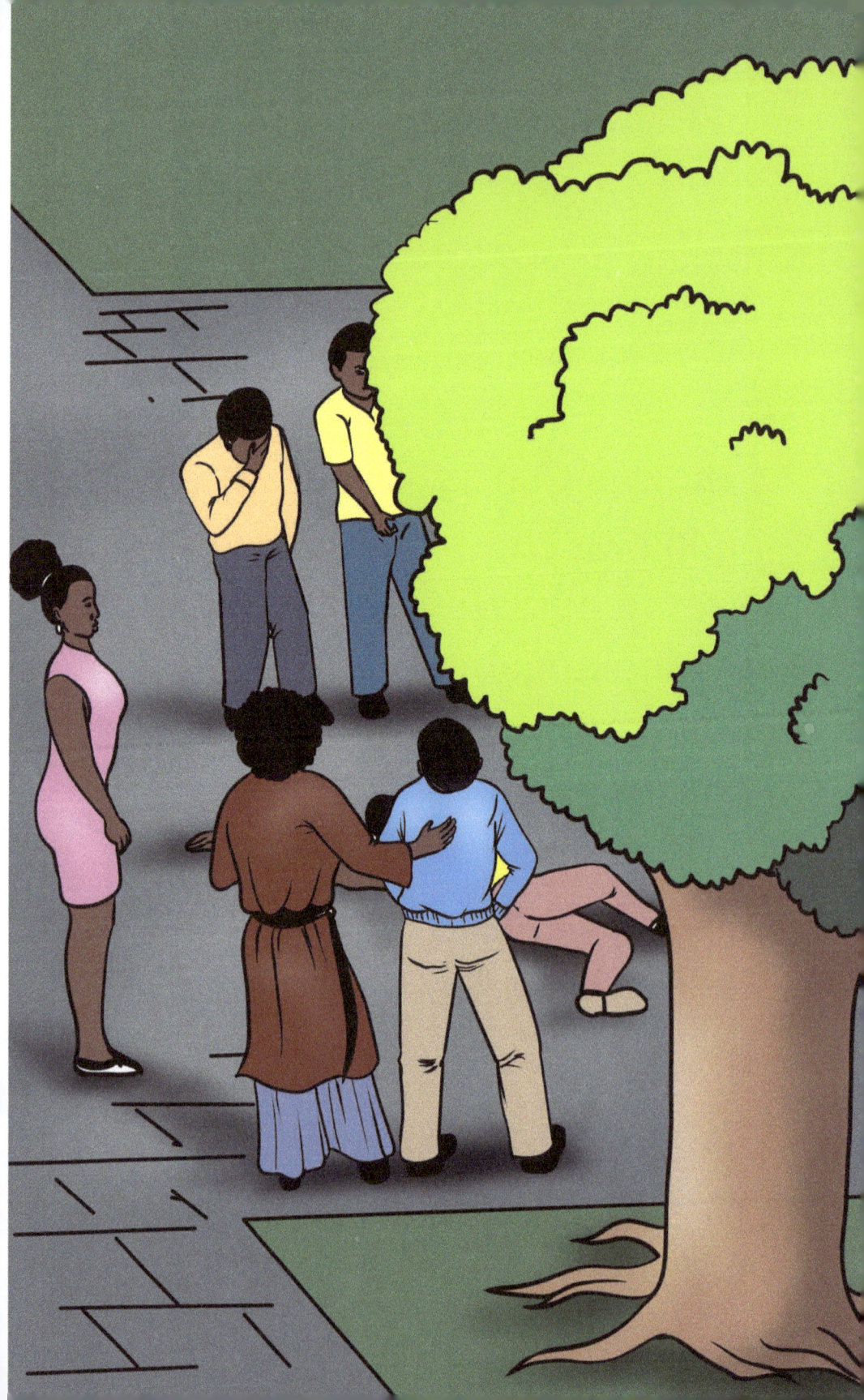

Suddenly, he saw a crowd of people shouting. He wondered what was going on and what they were looking at. When he got closer, he saw a man on the ground who was hurt. Someone had attacked him.

Cherry Wood ran away in fear.

He was frightened and began to cry.

He found his tree friends and they asked, "Why are you crying Cherry Wood?" "I saw something that hurt my heart and when I tried to forget about it, it just keeps coming back to my mind," Cherry Wood told them. "I just can't forget what I saw."

The tree friends began to cry too and one asked Cherry Wood, "Did you tell anyone about it?"

"No, said Cherry Wood, it's hard for me to talk about it... I'm scared. I don't feel so good."

Cherry Wood's tree friends told him, "You're not alone," one tree said, "I know... maybe Mr. Oak can help. He will help you through your tough time." Another tree said, "Yeah...he listens and always seems to come up with wise words."

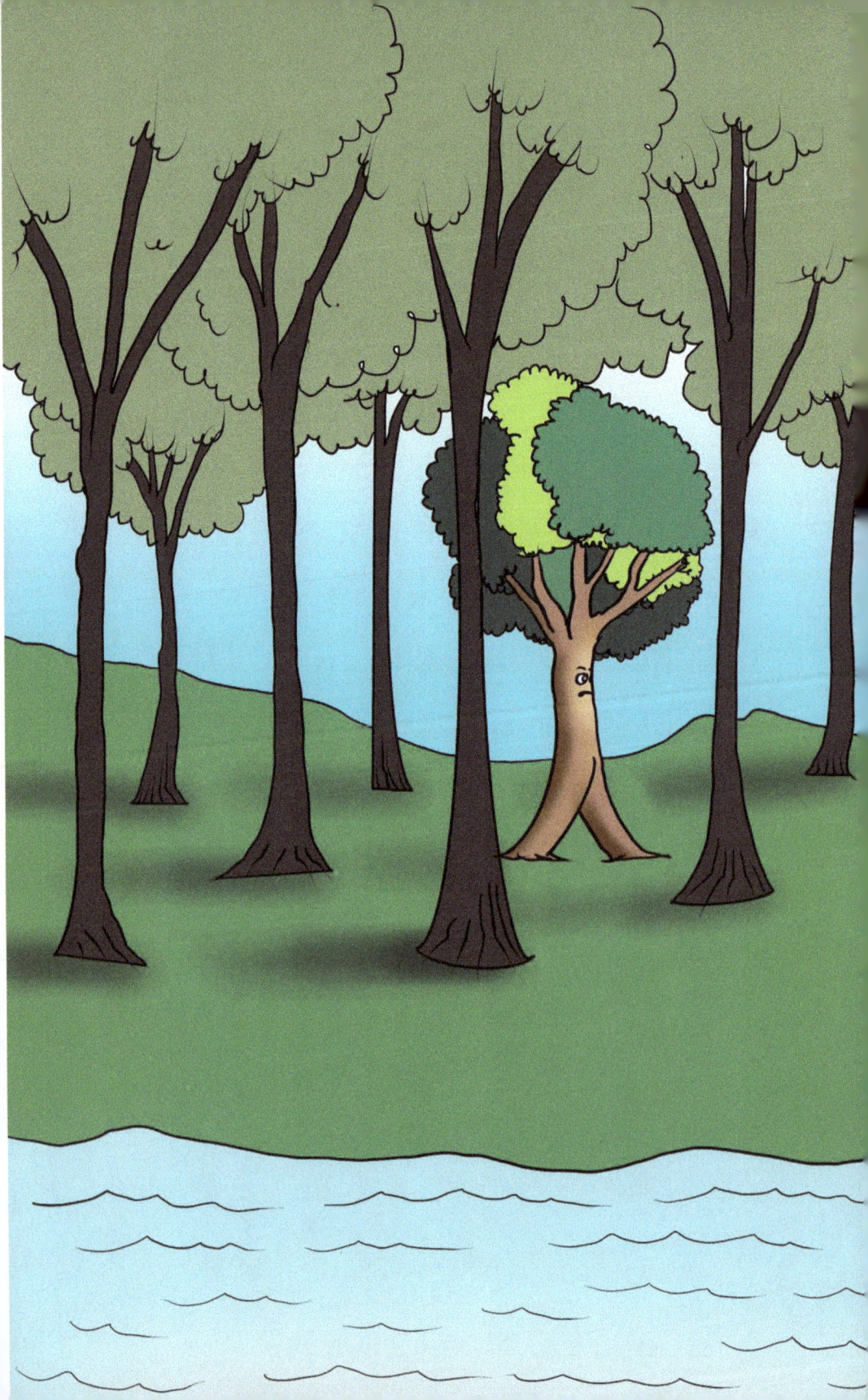

Cherry Wood nodded, "Yes I guess so...."

So Cherry Wood took off to find Mr. Oak.

He looked everywhere and couldn't find him. He thought, Mr. Oak always shows up at unexpected times. He remembered when Mr. Oak surprised him at his birthday party, and another time when he bumped into him after being bullied and lost.

He thought, "Hum, where is Mr. Oak?" He sat down on a rock and began to cry; he was feeling alone and scared.

He couldn't stop thinking of the man on the ground, hurt. Cherry Wood thought. "Is this going to happen to me too? Will I be the next one to be hurt? I can't seem to forget what I saw; it frightens me," and he cried even more.

All of a sudden, out of nowhere, Mr. Oak was standing right in front of him. Cherry Wood lifted his head in surprise!

Mr. Oak said, "I heard and felt your cry. Your sadness touched my heart, and I came running as fast as I could to find you."

Cherry Wood was so happy to see Mr. Oak.

Mr. Oak said, "How can I help dry your tears?" Cherry Wood said, "I'm so sad..." Mr. Oak asked, "Why are you so sad?"

Cherry Wood explained that he had seen a man on the ground hurt and that he kept seeing it over and over in his mind. "I don't know what to do to make it go away," said Cherry Wood and tears ran down his cheeks.

Mr. Oak said to himself,
"This is traumatic...hum,"
and he turned to comfort
Cherry Wood, "I understand
your fears and feel your pain
Cherry Wood," Mr. Oak said,
"Let's go for a walk together
and you can tell me all about
it."

So Cherry Wood walked and talked to Mr. Oak, and Mr. Oak listened. They took many walks together after that.

Cherry Wood began to feel better each time they walked and talked.
Mr. Oak cared, and he gave good advice.

Mr. Oak explained to Cherry Wood, that there are good people that help others, and there are not-so-good people who hurt others.

He said, "Set yourself free, do not carry this burden. Cherry Wood tried hard to forget how he was feeling.

Sometime later, Mr. Oak took Cherry Wood to a clinic where he could get even more help. A place where he could get free from his unhappy thoughts, so Cherry Wood could be happy again!

The End

For More information or ordering.

Please email to:

chloeartspublishing@gmail.com

or check your online bookstores.

"Understanding our world from a child's perspective"
Dr. Joyce Marrie

www.ingramcontent.com/pod-product-compliance
Lightning Source LLC
Chambersburg PA
CBHW050843270326
41930CB00019B/3456